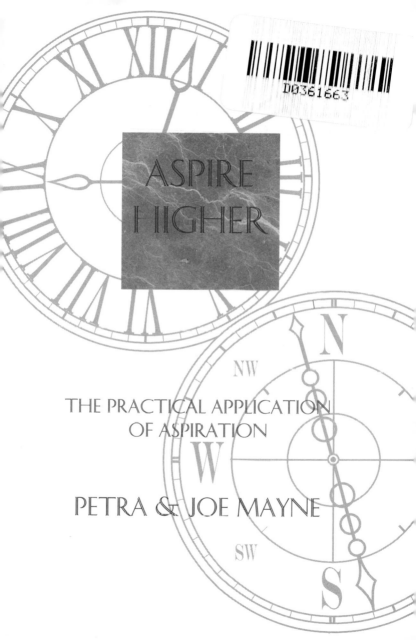

ASPIRE HIGHER

THE PRACTICAL APPLICATION OF ASPIRATION

PETRA & JOE MAYNE

ISBN: 1-890676-93-4

Library of Congress Catalog Card Number: 00-111614

First Printing:
Printed in the United States of America

04 03 02 01 00 6 5 4 3 2 1

Editing by Doug Benson
Typesetting By Mori Studio
Edina, MN 55439

Address orders to:
Beaver's Pond Press
5125 Danen's Drive
Edina, Minnesota 55439-1465
(952)829-8818

For Spencer, Connor, & Amanda

*Who are our daily inspiration
to aspire higher.*

We love you.

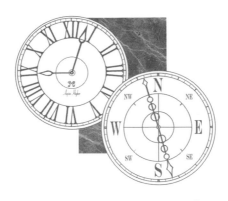

CONTENTS

INTRODUCTION

What makes for a truly exceptional life? Peace, Grace, Wealth, Title, Admiration, Affection, Respect, Power, Contentment?

We've put together a perspective on leveraging your aspirations so they provide you with an exceptional life. *Aspire Higher* focuses on the "High Five"—five key areas that, we are confident, make up the basic elements of a full, rich existence when they are carefully nurtured.

These five areas are:

- · Your relationships.
- · Your spirituality.

- · Your career choices.
- · Your financial resources and how you handle them.
- · Your health—both physical and mental.

How you choose to deal with each of these will largely determine your ultimate level of happiness and fulfillment.

Aspirations and Goals

In the presentations we do for associations, businesses and schools, we define the difference between setting goals and defining Aspirations.

Goals are important, and establishing them is a key step in achieving your greater good. But look at goals as tactics, the day-to-day checklist of things you wish to accomplish. This list is a dynamic document and should be changed as your life unfolds. Goals are simply the milestones you'll use to assess the progress of your journey.

Aspirations are goals applied. They are the strategic portion of your plan. Aspirations are the view from 30,000 feet. They provide greater direction and purpose. They inspire you and drive you. Aspirations are not just lofty goals. They can literally define you as a person.

This book is a guide to the practical application of aspirations: Goals ratcheted up a notch, dreams realized, destiny defined.

To aspire, to breathe deeply of life, and to set an example for others through our accomplishments and struggles, is to add another dimension to our years.

Questioning

In our experience, intelligent people continually strive to better themselves. They aren't complacent about their station in life; they seek avenues to improve their lot.

This isn't to say that these folks can't be pleased or are never happy. It means that they have a "healthy discontent," a mild irritation with the status quo.

Researchers who've studied Generation X (the group, now in their 20s and 30s, that came after the Baby Boomers) have often identified this trait with this "lost" demographic group. Observers note that, "They ['Gen Xers'] never seem to be happy with where they are," or ask, "Why can't Xers just stay put for even 6 months?" Many Human Resources professionals share this frustration with the Xers' restlessness.

But it's not just Gen Xers who question the status quo; this vague dissatisfaction with things as they are is a state most of us reach in our lives, regardless of the generation we were born into. The perspective we gain (often in our late 20's to early 30's) allows us to view our lives "from 30,000 feet." We pull back and view not just the road, but where the road leads. We start to understand landmarks and mile markers. We make choices that sometimes lead us down rough roads or roads with obstacles.

It also is a time when we realize that those "easy" choices, those easy roads we took in our inexperienced youth, may not have taken us to positive places.

Why would anyone take a path, no matter how easy it seemed, without knowing where it would lead? Because, not having been born with wisdom and experience, we've had to!

None of us was ever handed a completed life map. We were taught how to read a map, how to use a compass and how to ask for directions. But we have to create the route, "blaze the trail," for ourselves.

The Compass

When you take pause (moments, mostly) and wonder, "Am I going where I want to go? Am I becoming what I want to become?" these questions relate exactly to this sense of uneasiness everyone feels at one time or another. This is not necessarily a mid-life crisis, nor boredom, nor the uncertain search for ultimate meaning reflected in questions such as, "Why am I here?" or Who am I?" Instead, these are questions asked with confidence. "I actually could continue existing the way I am now. But what else is there for me to do? What other ways can I contribute that will enable me to grow?"

You're beyond looking at the surface of the road. You know it's sometimes clear and sometimes has obstacles. You know it can be smooth or rough, downhill or uphill.

Now you're looking at the lay of the land. You have an aerial view. You pull out your compass.

But these are not minor undertakings. *Should* you question your life? Look at your parents or others around you. Shouldn't you just be grateful for what you have? "If it's not broke…"

We've been programmed by past generations who have known war and scarcity. These learned and wise elders remember a time of less abundance and less permissiveness, when material security was precarious and achieving even the most modest goals required strict discipline.

Most of those who lived through World War II and/or the Great Depression value the lessons of those times but wouldn't wish the hardships or pain they experienced on anyone.

It's a natural human desire to want to better your existence, not necessarily by acquiring more things, but by enhancing your skills and abilities, and by accepting more and greater challenges in order to grow.

Once you've mastered traversing the road, you can look up to see if you're going in the right direction. That's what these questions are: a response to a point in your life when you sense in yourself an as-yet untapped capacity for growth.

Using the compass allows you to break away from the day-to-day routines and look at a broader view. The new perspective is more strategic, less tactical.

In addition to your compass, there is one more piece of vital gear.

The Clock

As the compass guides you, the clock keeps you on task. It reminds you to plan quickly. Plan with some urgency. The clock doesn't stop.

Going in the direction of your dreams, achieving your destiny, acting on your aspirations takes both a clock and a compass.

Decide on your direction but don't take too long! In order to achieve, you must DO! Once you're on your way, you'll have positive momentum working with you.

The clock doesn't stop. It serves as a constant reminder to move.

Is it the clock that makes us question our current position in the first place? Is it the sudden realization that our time on earth is finite that motivates us to get out of bed in the morning, to think about the importance of growth and change?

Is time that valuable? Just look at how we refer to time. It's more than valuable. It's the ultimate treasure. You can waste time, steal a moment, invest your time, save time. Just like money. Unlike money, however, you cannot earn more of it. And what's gone you can never get back.

In an article in Fast Company Magazine (Jan.–Feb. 2000), Gina Imperato writes about "The Money Value of Time." She explores how we all know the time value of money…but what if we were able to leverage our "down time" in exchange for cash?

The clock is a constant reminder to act. For those who aspire higher, it's most effective to use a clock and a compass.

THE PRESENT

Imagine there is a bank that credits your account each morning with $86,400. It carries over no balance from day to day. Every evening the bank deletes whatever part of the balance you failed to use during the day. What would you do? Draw out every cent, of course!

Each of us has such a bank. Its name is TIME. Every morning, it credits you with 86,400 seconds. Every night it writes off, as lost, whatever of this you have failed to invest to a good purpose. It carries over no balance. It allows no overdraft. Each day it opens a new account for you. Each night it burns the remains of the day. If you fail to use the day's deposits, the loss is yours. There is no going back. There is no drawing against the "tomorrow." You must live in the present on today's deposits. Invest it so as to get from it the utmost in health, happiness and success.

The clock is running. Make the most of the day.

To realize the value of ONE YEAR, ask a student who failed a grade.

To realize the value of ONE MONTH, ask a mother of a premature baby.

To realize the value of ONE WEEK, ask the editor of a weekly newspaper.

To realize the value of ONE HOUR, ask the lovers who are waiting to meet.

To realize the value of ONE MINUTE, ask a person who missed the train.

To realize the value of ONE SECOND, ask a person who just avoided an accident.

To realize the value of ONE MILLISEC-OND, ask the person who won the Silver Medal in the Olympics.

Treasure every moment that you have! And treasure it more because you shared it with someone special, special enough to spend your time. And remember time waits for no one. Yesterday is history. Tomorrow is mystery. Today is a gift. That's why we call it the present!

—Author unknown

NOTES

ASPIRE HIGHER

NOTES

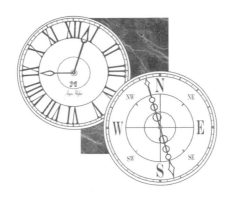

RELATIONSHIPS

"We are each of us angels with only one wing. And we can only fly embracing each other."

—*Luciano de Crescenzo*

"Everything that lives lives not alone nor for itself."

—*William Blake*

The fullness of life involves interaction with other people. While this is often a difficult and even painful area for many, it is the most rewarding as well.

Like anything of value, relationships require the investment of effort, attention, time and other resources. Nurturing friendships, finding a life-long companion add multiple dimensions to experiencing the joys of our existence.

Is having great wealth worth it if you have no one to share its benefits with?

The thought of being forever alone can chill you to the marrow.

Relationships—whether intimate, casual, familial, or work-related—all exist at different levels and you get out of them what you put into them.

And true, deep, lasting relationships all take time to develop and nurture.

The people with whom you associate can have a powerful effect on your level of success. Research has shown that people's bank accounts tend to be at about the same level as those of the people they spend most of their time with.

A shared view is a powerful force. Do your friends and confidants support you in your dreams? Do they help keep you on task?

The power of your aspirations can be felt by those around you. It may create some jealousy. You have drive, conviction, direction and purpose. Look around. Do your associates have a similar approach to life or are they just ticking off the days to the future that they hope works out?

Take a good look.

Share your life of love and abundance and joy and giving. It can't be done alone. Spend the time developing.

LIFE-LONG LEARNING

 ASK

- Are the people I associate with contributing to my successes, or are they hindering my growth?
- What groups share my interests, values, aspirations?
- How do I add value to my relationships?

 ACT

- Make a date with my spouse.
- Be the first to call to mend a grudge with a friend.
- Read an extra bedtime story to my children tonight.

RESOURCES

Don't Sweat the Small Stuff with Your Family, by Richard Carlson, Ph.D.

NOTES

NOTES

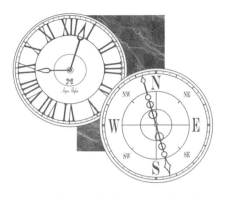

SPIRITUALITY

"Faith has to do with things that are not seen, and hope with things that are not in hand."

—Saint Thomas Aquinas

"There are only two ways to live your life. One is as though nothing is a miracle: The other is as though everything is a miracle."

—Albert Einstein

People of great accomplishment attribute some portion of their success to a connection with a "higher power." It isn't necessarily "divine intervention" that is the reason for goal attainment, but the strength and comfort that spirituality brings.

Doctors and counselors point to down time for thinking or reflection as crucial to long-term health. We feel that taking time to contemplate or meditate allows the brain to solve problems both big and small.

A key problem-solving technique is as simple as "sleeping on it," letting your mind "percolate" and work through things subconsciously. Is this spirituality?

Whether you call it prayer, meditation, quiet time or something else, this contemplative break is a vital facet of aspiration. Solidifying your thoughts and firming up your resolve brings your goals and aspirations closer to reality.

Some define spirituality as a place where they find their place or purpose. Others say it is where they get their energy. Are you comfortable with your beliefs? We strongly believe that this cannot be overlooked. Spirituality becomes your moral compass and helps you identify the legacy you'll leave.

> *"It's only when we truly know and understand that we have a limited time on earth—and that we have no way of knowing when our time is up—that we will begin to live each day to the fullest, as if it was the last one we had."*
>
> *—Elizabeth Kubler-Ross*

LIFE-LONG LEARNING

 ASK

- How did spirituality/religion (or lack of it) affect me during my childhood?
- What questions do I have about my own faith/religion/spirituality?
- What am I thankful for today?

 ACT

- Bring my list to a spiritual advisor to discuss answers.
- Write a personal mission statement.
- Keep a Journal...even of just one thing that made me smile or wonder each day.

RESOURCES

Experiencing God, by Henry T. Blackaby & Claude V. King

The Road Less Traveled, by M. Scott Peck, M.D.

Simple Abundance: a daybook of comfort and joy, by Sarah Ban Breathnach

NOTES

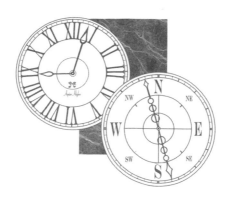

CAREER CHOICES

"The majority work to make a living; some work to acquire wealth or fame, while a few work because there is something within them which demands expression...only a few truly love it."
—*Edmond Boreaux Szekely*

The Job-Career-Vocation Progression

This concept is key in bringing one's aspirations into focus.

Defining your job, moving on to understanding your career, and then advancing your aspirations to vocation can be a powerful life planning tool.

Let's begin.

A job is defined as a specific, finite task or set of tasks. It has a distinct beginning and end. You are able to identify very clearly what your job is.

The set of tasks or defined parameters usually can be summed up in how you would respond to the question; "What do you do for a living?"

Your answer is very telling. We all have held jobs. The new economy mandates that workers who are starting out now will have many different jobs. In the not-too-distant past, an individual who held several jobs in, say, a five-year period, was said to be "job-hopping." Most people assumed that the job-hopper "just couldn't hold a job."

Times have changed. Today, we would question anyone who has held the same job for more than 18 months to two years. If we were evaluating them for employment we would ask, "How have you grown in these many months? How has this job helped you to develop your skills?"

If they stayed the same during this tenure, then they regressed.

So a job is a specific task or set of tasks.

A career is a series of jobs that have a common thread. In fact the origin of the word "career" comes from the French word for "cart" or "track". You've heard of someone on a career track? Or path?

In the typical working lifetime, many, if not most, individuals will have multiple careers. Usually each career will center around the skills that person possesses.

You can have dozens of jobs. You can have multiple careers. But what about a vocation?

The very definition comes from the Latin word "vocare," or, "to call." Your vocation is your calling. It is what you were meant to do.

We define your vocation as what you would do if money weren't an issue. It's what you would do for free. Often it's working with a skill set that you are comfortable with. What you are a natural at.

The Job-Career-Vocation progression is a powerful journey to undertake. During that journey, you will uncover much about your motivations and your path to fulfillment.

As you aspire higher, you need to discover an answer to the question, "What would you do for free?" Ask this of your managers and of the people you hire. Their answers will reveal a lot about what drives them and what is important to them.

Shouldn't we all aspire toward our calling? Don't we all need to reach for that end?

New Workplace/New Workforce

Today's marketplace demands a certain degree of comfort with uncertainty. Gone are the days when you signed on with a company and progressed thorough the ranks until you retired 40 years later.

The market doesn't allow for that "cog" mentality anymore. Employees can't guarantee they'll stay with a company and Employers can't guarantee that the market will provide lifelong jobs.

This is not a reflection of the evil of corporations or of a lack of loyalty by workers. It is merely a fact of the new economy.

Skilled workers understand that, today, opportunity with a firm is project-based. They will work until their portion of a project is finished and then move on.

Soon benefits and retirement will be so portable that "free-lancing" will become the norm, not the exception.

Workers will have many employers simultaneously and won't be burdened with corporate superstructures and bureaucracies that can stifle creativity and productivity.

The only "safety net" for workers is their individual skill level. You need to remain marketable and flexible. You will choose who you work with or for and under what conditions.

Employers, likewise, can select who they work with based on the project to be completed or the merit of your past work.

This is the marketplace at its best: keeping the worthy properly rewarded and inspiring everyone to continually improve.

LIFE-LONG LEARNING

 ASK

· Am I leveraging all of my skills and attributes to attract income opportunities?
· Am I in a field of endeavor that will move me toward my wealth goals?

 ACT

· Update my resume.
· Keep a "Brag-able Binder" full of any accolades earned or awards won throughout my professional life.
· Make frequent contact with my mentor a priority.
· Offer to become a mentor.

RESOURCES

Do What You Love, the Money Will Follow, by Marsha Sinetar

Blur: The Speed of Change in the Connected Economy, by Christopher Meyer and Stan Davis

Fast Company magazine

NOTES

NOTES

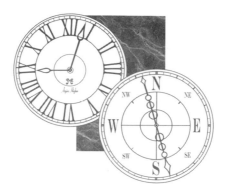

FINANCES AND ABUNDANCE

"It's not hard to make a lot of money, if alls you want to do is make a lot of money."

—from the film Citizen Kane

"Prosperity is living easily and happily in the real world, whether you have money or not."

—Jerry Gillies

One of the greatest sources of stress in our society is finances, making sure there is always enough income to meet one's needs. Keeping this vital concern in balance with the rest of your life is key to successful living. Having financial aspirations means identifying how you will accumulate wealth in order to live a full life.

Money provides freedom to spend precious time pursuing your dreams and creating your legacy. Again-look at your financial picture from a distance.

Thoughts on Quick Money

It is the opportunity to add or create value for someone else that allows us to add to our wealth. Rarely—very rarely—is this done easily or quickly.

We've seen to too many rueful individuals who have fallen for the easy money or quick money pitch. They've lost thousands of their "security" dollars in the hope of gaining fast, easy returns.

Our economy's growth is based on the ability and willingness of people to take prudent risks, and there are many investments worth acting on after the proper research is done. Successful people aspire to secure their future by filling the needs of others. You may be attracted by the lure of short-term gains, but keep in mind that the marketplace determines ultimate value.

Establishing a solid financial plan puts you at ease. It frees up creative energy to focus on establishing and enhancing relationships and building your career. Money is not an end in itself, but it is a necessary part of a full, rich life.

> *"There is serious defect in the thinking of someone who wants—more than any-thing else—to become rich. As long as they don't have the money, it'll seem like a worthwhile goal. Once, they do, they'll understand how important other things are—and always have been."*
> —Joseph Brooks

LIFE-LONG LEARNING

 ASK

- Am I able to invest at a rate that will give me/my family the security I/we need?
- Do I have a wealth accumulation plan? (this would come after a debt reduction plan).
- Can I identify and use the wealth enhancement tools the market provides?

 ACT

- Make a will.
- Make an appointment with a financial planner.
- Get out of debt.
- Invest whatever I can.

RESOURCES

The Richest Man in Babylon, by Napoleon Hill

A Random Walk Down Wall Street, by Burton Gordon Malkiel

NAIC (National Association of Investors Corporation)

NOTES

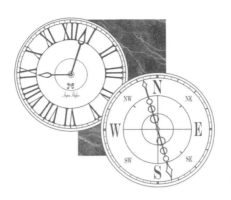

HEALTH AND WELLNESS

" A man needs a purpose for real health."
—Sherwood Anderson

Physical Health

If there is one facet of a "life abundant" that we constantly struggle with, it is health. In this time of rapidly advancing technology, when work is increasingly more knowledge-based and is defined in terms of mental effort rather than physical labor, becoming sedentary is far too easy.

We are not here to provide an exercise regimen or secrets to fitness. But the successful people we've studied have made health and wellness more than just idle words.

Aspiration requires drive, focus and determination. It will require you to maintain a high level of energy. Carefully selecting the foods you eat and establishing disciplined fitness habits will help bring you to this energy level.

Like finances, however, fitness is only one of several aspects of life and must be kept in balance with the others. There are some who have jumped headfirst into the "if I exercise, I'll live forever" craze. We have seen too many people strive for immortality only to be left with a legacy of little accomplishment.

For centuries successful people have understood the need for a healthful existence. It comes with a balance of good food, preventive medicine, exercise and discipline.

In fact, the "passion" for fitness and the drive to force one's appearance into some culturally "desirable" form can often increase your stress level or distract you from pursuing your greater aspirations.

No one feels perfect all the time. The body needs proper rest, sustenance, and exercise. If you have not experienced the physical (and mental, in our opinion) benefits of a full body massage by a trained therapeutic masseuse, you are missing one of the great pleasures in life.

You will find that a physical feeling of well-being is closely tied to your mental health and attitude.

Mental Health and Attitude

The power of a positive mental attitude is probably the most important factor in aspirational thinking. It's based on feeling good about yourself, feeling self-confident.

Identifying and appreciating your level of comfort with yourself speaks volumes. It is manifested in a level of confidence that literally draws people to you.

Positive people are a pleasure to be around and their positive mental attitude attracts opportunity as well. It is not an accident or a fallacy that positive things happen to positive people.

When you are upbeat and focus on the good in the world, you will be amazed at how your life changes for the better. You can also think of being positive as being someone who adds to situations and relationships.

Attitude = "Added To"

We've all met people who are the opposite of this—people who are literally negative—who only take from others and look out for their own personal gain at every opportunity. Just being around them drains you of your energy.

How would others describe you? Are you a positive, forward-thinking person? Do you have a ready smile and a sense of good cheer?

There is a program within the Boy Scouts of America in which fellow Scouts choose the "best" among their peers to join the "Order of the Arrow." This group-within-a-group has many functions, ranging from preserving the outdoor camping experience to doing community service. But what impresses me most about the young people in this group is their focus on keeping a cheerful disposition no matter what— even in the midst of lousy jobs and burdensome responsibilities.

Teaching this principle can have only good results.

Everyone goes through moods. But if you wear them on your sleeve or let them dominate your disposition, you'll find people avoiding you.

A solid, healthy opinion of yourself, will lead to a level of comfort within yourself. And that can only result in higher aspirations.

"Finish each day and be done with it.
You have done what you could.
Some blunders and absurdities no doubt
crept in.
Forget them as soon as you can.
Tomorrow is a new day;
Begin it well and serenely
And with a high spirit
Not to be encumbered with your old non-
sense."

—Ralph Waldo Emerson

LIFE-LONG LEARNING

 ASK

· When is the last time I felt really healthy & fit?
· Am I letting past experiences have negative control over my life?
· What healthful habits have I incorporated into my life recently?
· Which lifestyle habits cause harm to my body or mind?

 ACT

· Schedule a thorough physical examination with my doctor.
· Consider seeking professional help with any persistent emotional issues.
· Enlist available resources to change unhealthy habits.
· Move!

NOTES

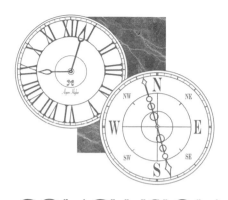

CONCLUSION:
LEAVING A LEGACY

We've now shared with you our thoughts on what we feel are the five key areas of life—the High Five. We've also given you "the compass"—points for reflection and direction—and "the clock"—specific actions and resources to make the most of these areas. The rest is up to you.

Please consider now, if it hasn't already crossed your mind, how maximizing these areas will leave a lasting legacy-your legacy.

By "legacy" we mean the whole constellation of things we leave behind-attitudes, memories, lessons, achievements, material wealth-so that those who come after us will benefit from our efforts. If this comes in the form of positive achievements or as the result of struggle, it is the greatest gift we can give beyond living fully and well.

In our relationships, if they're lovingly nurtured and genuine, we can know that our friends or siblings or children will have had an outstanding example of how to love and to care. They will have seen through us how to handle life's tough times and come out a better person in the end. They will have a positive blueprint for their future and the future of all they come in contact with.

Spiritually, what greater gift can we give ourselves and those around us than an understanding of why we are here and how we fit into the grand scheme of things? Values such as love, honesty, forgiveness, and service can become reality to those around us.

Making a life rather than making a living is the key to leaving a legacy in the area of our careers. It's not the income, but the work ethic and setting an example of how one can grow and serve "on the job" that matters. It's also the searching journey of our calling that can be most rewarding to us and inspirational to others.

Using our resources wisely and generously can make a lasting impact. Our financial legacy can be as simple as teaching the young the benefits of thrift or as grandiose as building a library for future generations to use and enjoy. The accumulation of wealth for the sake of wealth is an empty goal. Abundance that can be shared is the ultimate aspiration.

Finally, we must remember the importance of maintaining a healthy body and soul, which can truly allow us to experience an exceptional life. The gift of ourselves—our stories, lore and example—can mean much. Speaker and author Jim Rohn even urges us to leave our pictures and our libraries as a gift. A long life that is filled with thought and study and is highlighted with action and accomplishment will have a far wider and more lasting effect than any granite monument.

SUCCESS

To laugh often and much;
To win the respect
Of intelligent people
And the affection of children;
To earn the appreciation
Of honest critics and endure
The betrayal of false friends;
To appreciate beauty,
To find the best in others;
To leave the world
A bit better, whether
By a healthy child,
A garden patch
Or a redeemed social condition;
To know that even one life
Has breathed easier
Because you have lived.
That is to have succeeded.
                    —Ralph Waldo Emerson

NOTES

NOTES

ON YOUR JOURNEY . . .

You can inspire your friends and associates to Aspire Higher. Ask your local bookseller or visit Amazon.com. To order in volume, call our friend Milt Adams at Beaver's Pond Press: 952-741-8818.

And we'd like to hear from you! Send us your comments and thoughts and stories. You can be sure we'll credit you in our future publications.

The MAYNE Speaker
18998 Baldwin Street Northwest
Elk River, Minnesota 55330

aspirehigher@maynespeaker.com

All the best,
Petra and Joe Mayne

ASPIRE HIGHER LIVE!

The MAYNE Speaker is available for your group, company, or association. We work with colleges and universities nationwide to develop leaders for the marketplace and with businesses to seek out and hire those leaders.

You can implement these powerful insights. From keynote to full-day presentations . . . The MAYNE Speaker can take your group to new heights.

For booking details and availability, call us at 1-800-490-9781.